Courtr
& The

By Damien Enright

Timoleague Abbey

A Merlin Press Publication

Published by Merlin Press

ISBN 1 902631 00 5

Design by Sean O'Leary
Cover photos by Mick Browne
Frontispiece by Dan O'Connell
Illustrations by Steve J. Pawsey

MERLIN PRESS
Courtmacsherry, Co. Cork
Tel/Fax: +353 023 46045

Contents

Five easy, circular walks in West Cork's lovely scenery and clean air. Average distance from Cork, 25 miles, Kinsale 12, Bandon 8, Clonakilty 8.

Dedicated to

my patient wife, children, friends and dog,
who have made life's roads a pleasure
and lightened my steps on the way.

ALSO IN THIS SERIES

Walks in and around Kinsale
Walks of Clonakilty Town and Country
Walks of Ballydehob and Schull
Walks of Skibbereen, Baltimore and Roaringwater Bay

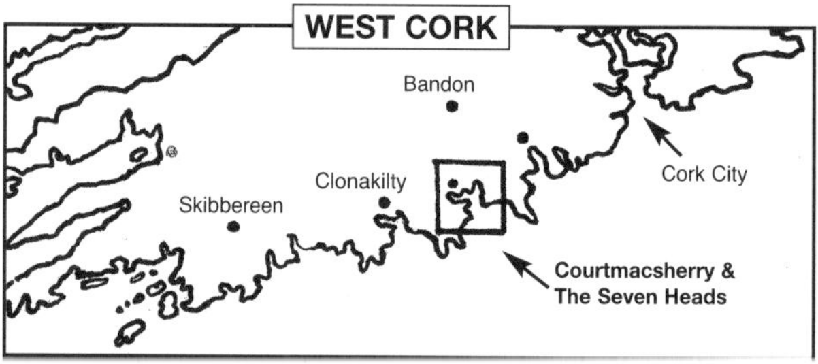

There is no guarantee that a walk outlined in this book is a right-of-way. The author and supporters of this book do not accept any responsibility for trespass nor for accident or loss to or by the public in walking these routes.

A note on walking

The Irish are big on walking. If there is one thing we have plenty of, it is back roads and fresh air.

There are the power walkers, the Walking Women of Ireland, plugging along country roads with hips and shoulders swinging, out for the exercise after an already much-exercised day. The glow of their cheeks and the litheness of their stride attests the beneficial effects of 'exercise walking'.

Irish men, on the other hand, seem oblivious to walking's cosmetic effect, an unfortunate oversight on their part. Males are not seen striding along country lanes. When we do see a male abroad, he is generally being pulled along at a heart-stopping pace by two fist-fulls of dog leads, his greyhounds taking him for a run, rather than the other way around. Other encounters will involve men in caps, with fags in mouth and pockets full of fivers, out following the road bowling, after which they will walk miles.

There are the hill walkers and long-distance route marchers, doughty folk in serious boots, with ashplants, maps and small rucksacks. To them, we owe the opening up of green roads and byways, and the mapping of mountain trails not trodden since the ancient Celts made their way across country via uplands, the plains being covered with a dense growth of trees.

I, myself, do not power walk, greyhound follow, or road bowl wager. I walk for the curiosity and the uplift, the wonderments of the wayside and the 'high' of the free-flowing endorphins released after twenty minutes on the hoof. I am not so much a slow walker as one who is waylaid by the roadside attractions. Curiosity, atmosphere or amazement delays me, and while the company forges ahead, I am left behind, in thrall.

The walks outlined in this book are for walkers such as I. They take, generally, just a couple of hours but can easily be stretched to fill half a day. They are perfect for a weekend afternoon or a holiday meander.

They will, hopefully, stimulate my perambulating neighbours towards new horizons and inform visitors of the lovely land that awaits just off the tourist trail. I cannot imagine these local by-ways ever becoming crowded. We may in time meet a party of ardent Japanese, led by a person with a flag, or stout Austrians in lederhosen and braces singing "Falderee-Falderah". They will be sure of a welcome. We Irish delight in showing off our land.

To the farmers and landowners

The land around Courtmacsherry and Barryroe is rich, and the farmers noted for their industry and enterprise. It has been maintained that their tradition of hard work was learned from the friars and lay brothers who worked outlying farms around the monasteries at Aghamanister, Abbeymahon and Timoleague. Others say it comes from the good grace of the Lords Barrymore who did not insist that tenants left their smallholdings to their eldest sons alone but allowed them to be divided between the brothers. Thus, all got land but many so little that to survive they had to work every hour God sent them. As a result, the present day Barryroe Coop farmers are noted as amongst the most productive in the land.

But for the goodwill of these farmers and landowners our enjoyment of their lovely landscape would be curtailed. Nine tenths of the walks here outlined are on lanes and back roads but roads do not always conveniently join up. To make circular routes, - where one does not have to return home by the way one came - I have found old tracks, well worn and still in daily use. I have spoken personally to the landowners and farmers whose ground is crossed. Universally, they have not only been co-operative, but wish well to the walker. But, they reasonably point out, if walkers cross their property, they must accept that they do so at their own risk.

It is not long since the Courtmacsherry/Seven Heads area lost its last native Irish speaker. The Irish tradition of courtesy and welcome to strangers still remains. I would like, hereby, to thank those land owners, Irish or from abroad, who uphold this tradition and put no let or hindrance to walkers using the time-honoured paths on their land.

The area

Courtmacsherry and the Seven Heads is replete with wonders and the only way to enjoy them is on the hoof. To walk is not to route-march; it is to relax and enjoy. The walks in this modest volume are all modest walks, accessible to anyone from five to eighty five in reasonable good health and spirits. Most are road walks, requiring no gate-climbing, barbed-wire-fence-crossing or mountaineering skills. The routes are chosen for their diversity. There is history here, nature there, beauty everywhere.

On the shores and hinterland of this little known peninsula only an hour from Cork, we have views and bracing air as heady as any in Ireland. We have historic remnants, landscapes and seascapes, cliffs and lush river valleys. We have the Gulf Stream climate, and soft weather which changes the view and may, sometimes, obscure it. We have seasons which, although gentle, alter everything. If we do not find the ranks of purple foxgloves standing like sentinels by the wayside, or the fuschia corridors, it is because it is the wrong time of year. But, in compensation, there may be toadstools in the forest, or kingfishers at the stream mouth, escaping the inland cold.

Spring and summer are wonderful in the old Courtmacsherry woods and on the Harbour View beaches and Dunworley sheltered coves. The back-road verges are a pallet of colours, the field rocks yellow with lichens, as if splattered with sea gulls eggs. Few experiences in life can be finer or more liberating than to sit on the cliffs at Coolim of a summer evening and watch the gannets plummeting into the sea.

But autumn and winter also have their breathtaking moments. Courtmacsherry village, in the slanting October light, with a mirror-calm bay in front and the red-topped woods behind, conjures a peace the traveller will go far to find No TV nature programme brings home the sharp air of November on the Seven Heads, with snorting seals and ravening birds feeding on the sprat shoals that fill Coolbaun Bay. No celluloid footage can lift one's heart as with a flock of three thousand golden plover climbing into the blue January sky. No recorded sound-bite is as exciting as the real-life cacophony of two thousand rooks opposite Timoleague Abbey, flying in curtains over the twilight sea.

It is to such special roadside attractions that I have tried to direct my readers. Walking is required for their enjoyment but the walks are short, sweet, and worthwhile.

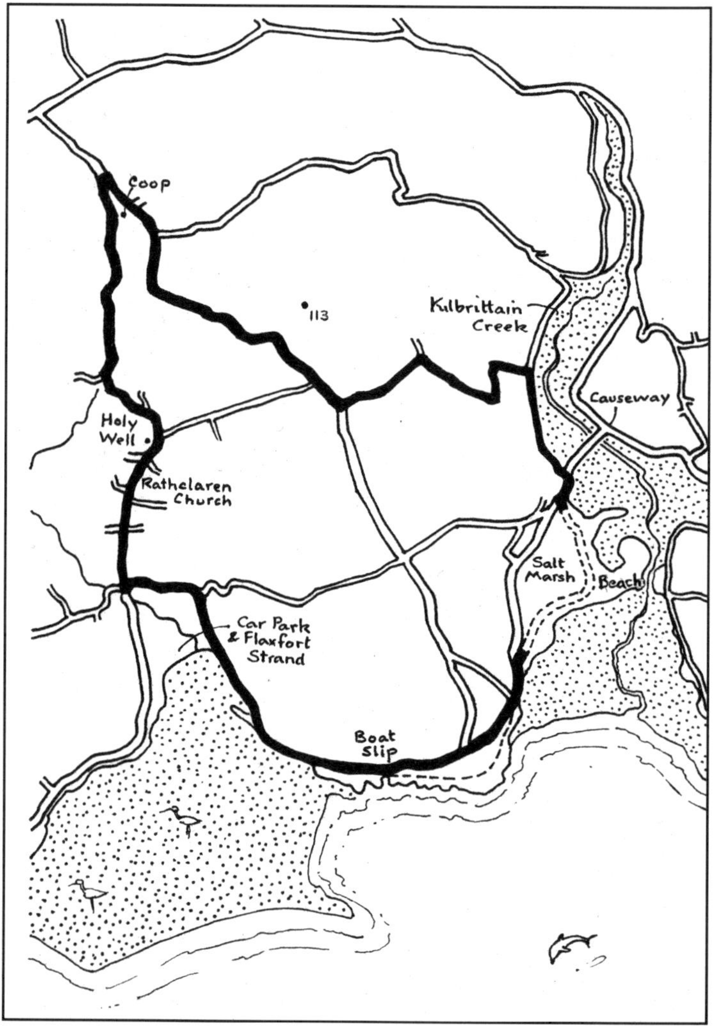

Walk No.1: Harbour View. 2.5 hours. About 5 miles.

Harbour View Walk

Flaxfort Pond and BirdWatch Ireland Reserve - historic church and medieval Holy Well - uplands, with elevated views over the bay - Kilbrittain River and creek - salt marshes, dunes and storm beach at Harbour View - a coastal path and rocky coves.

Locality: OS Map Sheet 87 Square 5245, the eastern side of Courtmacsherry Bay at Lisheenaleen and Harbour View. Bandon, 7 miles, Kinsale, 9.

Description and distance: A loop walk, 5 to 6 miles.

Walking Time: 2.5 hrs.

Walking conditions: Quiet back roads with few, if any, cars. Sand flats, dunes and beach. Cliff path and short section of secondary road with occasional cars. One incline, long, but very gradual.

Features: Five distinct wildlife habitats, each featuring different bird, animal and plant life. Historic church, graveyard and holy well. Country houses. Panoramic views of Courtmacsherry Bay. A storm beach, and dunes.

Flora and fauna: Flaxfort Pond is a BirdWatch Ireland reserve, and coots, herons, moor hens, reed buntings and four species of duck present much of the year. Ravens, yellowhammers and finches frequent the high ground Kilbrittain Creek is a major roost for many wader species, and kingfishers and otters may also be seen. Snipe abound on the salt marshes, and sky larks rise above the dunes. Grey plover and ring plover are seen on the strand, with occasional Brent geese, and swans. On the cliff walk, small flocks of choughs are a regular feature, with occasional sightings of kestrel and merlin. The rocks pools contain a variety of sea algaes, shellfish, crustaceans, anemones and small fish. Viviparous lizards bask on the stone walls on sunny summer days.

Equipment: Comfortable walking shoes.

Itinerary

(1) We set off from the small car park at Flaxfort Strand. The 'fort' derives from the local Irish name 'Lisheenaleen' [lios, a fort] and the 'flax' may come from the crop grown there when the name was translated into English. Nearby Timoleague was a centre of linen weaving, for which flax was the raw material. There are picnic tables, and when the tide is in, children swim off this beach, the water never exceeding a depth of a few feet. A small stream crosses the beach from the pond and contains sticklebacks, pond skaters and water boatmen. In summer, small flatfish and eels enter the steam, part of their early life cycle.

Turning left out of the car park, we walk along the road skirting Flaxfort Pond. Good views of the BirdWatch Ireland Reserve are available. As many as twelve herons may be roosting on the islands and, in summer, coots, moorhens and reed buntings nest amongst the reeds. The trees along the edges are alder, favourites of siskins, which hang acrobatically from the catkins as they feed.

Passing the first turn right, we take the second, 200 yards along, and walk up a rising road between tall trees. To the left, we pass two tree lined drives leading to large houses, with park lands alongside the road. The second, a Queen Anne villa, may be glimpsed through the trees. The centre portion was built in 1720 by the Scott family who came to Ireland with Cromwell. The Scotts still own the surrounding land, the lower house and the large farmyard opposite.

Higher up, we pass the vicarage, set amongst trees and gardens beside the Holy Trinity Church, built in 1650 as a Reformed Church, probably on the site of a medieval chapel. While many Church of Ireland farmers and landowners live in the area - a legacy of Bandon's status as an English and staunchly Protestant town for over 200 years - the congregation has much reduced in recent times. Catholics and Protestants are buried in the cemetery alongside, amongst them an Irish romantic novelist, Donn Byrne. Returned from America, he bought Coolmain Castle (now the property of Walt Disney's nephew) after winning £2,000 on the tables at Monte Carlo. He was drowned when he accidentally drove into the bay, circa 1929.

On the left, we come to Holy Trinity Well, down a short, well kept lane. Shaped like a beehive hut, six feet in diameter and six feet high, the interior

Rathclaren Church

is mossy and cool, like a small cave. Opposite the entrance is a shelf, upon which stands a vase with flowers - albeit plastic - and a statue of the Virgin. A 'holy well' since medieval times, it was a place of pilgrimage, until - so the story goes - a fight between two bands of travelling people resulted in a death. It was cursed by the local priest and pilgrimages were made no more.

Continuing, we ignore the small road veering to the right, and pass three bungalows. Views are of big fields, divided by stately trees, with hills in the distance and a glimpse of the sea. In spring time, there is the coconut smell of gorse. On sunny banks, celandine glitters like gold dust. Primroses peek from the green undergrowth and wild daffs toss their heads in the breeze. The road winds through a small copse of pines, then past a small stone bridge and a ferny gorge of gorse and brambles, with ivy-grown trees climbing the steep slopes on either side.

We reach a minor upland, with rough grass and a small plantation of conifers, and then 'the creamery', a depot of Barryroe Coop, one of the largest farmers' co-operatives in Ireland. We turn sharp right at the T-junction, down behind the creamery, now walking south towards the sea.

(2) We ignore a road to the left and continue due south. We are unlikely to meet any traffic on this road, which affords us magnificent views of Courtmacsherry Bay far below and the multi-coloured sea-facing village across the water. "All on one side, like Courtmac", a saying goes. On winter evenings, smoke curls from the chimneys against the background of the woods of the Earl of Shannon estate and, at night, the village lights stretch almost a mile along the water. At the highest point, we can see both headlands at the bay mouth, Coolmain Point, on this side, and Wood Point opposite, with Barry's Point, further south, beyond.

We take the next turning left - the second left since leaving the creamery -

and as we descend, we see, to the south, Coolmain Beach and Coolmain Castle, with trees around. We are now walking downhill, towards Kilbrittain Creek, the road a dusty bohreen, little used, with few houses. We pass a group of old farmhouses on the left, with red-roofed barns, stone outbuildings and ruins. The ivy on the roadside walls is heavy with fat, black berries, important food for hungry Scandanavian and Russian thrushes that arrive with us in winter. On sunny days, the leaves shine like they have been shellacked. Dog violets bloom amongst the roadside daisies in springtime, and rabbits are common in the fields.

(3) We come out onto a big view. To the left, we may look up the course of the Kilbrittain River, with plantations of conifers and rough land in the valleys. Below us, is the causeway on the R600 road, crossing the river and the slob. The vista of the estuary, beach and sea beyond is magnificent. The river is a series of steams, winding through mud banks, often changing channels, so that its pattern is never twice the same. The mud flats shine, and are often very beautiful, mirroring the sky, the trees, even the birds, doubling everything up. Low islands of reeds are roosts for densely packed curlews, gulls, lapwing, widgeon and teal.

We descend very steeply, past a country guest house, and may hear the bubbling calls of the curlews before we reach the edge of Kilbrittain Creek, below. At the creek, we turn right along the quiet road that skirts the muddy edges, walking, now, towards the sea. Even if the large winter flocks of golden plover, lapwing and widgeon are absent, small numbers of redshanks, curlews and oystercatchers will be there in any season, the latter sharp black-and-white in the sun. Little Egrets, pretty, pure white storks which first nested in Ireland in 1997, in County Cork, can often be seen here, as can kingfishers, particularly when hard winters and frozen inland waters drive them to the sea. Otters are frequently seen in the pool in front of the bridge arches. Broken mussel shells litter the road - there is a large mussel bed underneath the bridge, and the hooded crows have learned to open them by dropping them onto the tarmac from on high. This might be construed as 'tool using', if one considers the road a tool. By the same rule, rocks would be tools for the lammergeier, the huge Pyrenean vulture whose name means 'bone-breaker' and who drops bones from a great height to break them for the marrow.

Reaching the causeway, we cross the road and walk right, and then leave the road immediately via a rough track that passes beside a pool and makes across a flat salt-marsh towards the dunes. If the tide is high, and the marsh flooded, we will have to walk further along the road to the car park to reach the beach.

The muddy stream which flows through the marsh is full of life, supporting clouds of small shrimp and prawns, dense as soup, sand gobies and small flatfish. Glassworth, saltworth, sandworth and scurvy grass are common plants of this environment, highly specialised to survive salt water and spray. From underfoot, snipe explode like rockets from the tussocks of rough grass and zig-zag out of range.

Flaxfort Pond

(4) The dunes are the home of the Banded Snail and the Great Black Slug, which also comes in bright orange and deep brown. In summer, caterpillars of the cinnabar moth, in black and amber stripes like the Kilkenny county colours, swarm over the yellow ragworth. The dunes are held together by marram grass, but sea holly, groundsel, hawkweed, herb robert and a host of other plants also bind the sand. The dunes move, and erosion invades the land. Elderly locals speak of a golf course where there is now wetland, and recall quite a different topography in their youth. Before the ready availability of ground limestone, fleets of lorries took sand away to spread on the land.

We cross the dunes, on a path if possible to save wear-and-tear on the precious marram, and reach the beach. The tide line will always be interesting, with flotsam, jetsam, sand hoppers and old boots. Nowadays, plastic is a scourge but a wide storm beach is usually scoured and almost pristine. One never knows what one will find on the high tide line - walkers have come upon baby seals, and stranded dolphins. The rotting kelp teems with sand

Swan landing, Kilbrittain Creek

fly and kelp fly, and thousands of sand hoppers and sea slaters leap and run in clouds when disturbed. Delicate shells of tellin, pink and shiny as baby's fingernails, are everywhere, with cockle shells, razor shells and clams.

If the tide is out, one may walk almost a half mile to the surf. The casts of lugworm dot the beach with small pyramids of exuded sand. The pattern of ripples on the hard sand is fascinating, and very beautiful. If it is windy day, the waves here can be spectacular and one can watch wind surfers, or body surfers, out amongst them - Harbour View beach, more properly called Garranafeen Strand, is a favourite venue. Flocks of birds, which include grey plover, with their distinctive large, dark eyes, often congregate on near the water's edge.

We walk towards the west end of the beach, and the car park field. Crossing this field, we exit through the gate onto the road and find a stile 50 yards along, immediately beyond the white house on the left. This stile accesses a pathway leading to the bottom of the field and an easy path that runs right above the sea. A pair of merlin - small hawks - hunts hereabouts, and may be glimpsed, the blue backed male, no bigger than a mistle thrush, or the larger, brown female, skimming over the grass and hedges.

(5) As we follow this path, by the good graces of the land owners, more and more of the opposite side of Courtmacsherry Bay is revealed - Horse Rock, where the seals congregate, Wood Point, and the woods of the Earl of Shannon estate, the hotel, and the village of variegated houses with the forest behind. This is a well-kept path, with stiles in the stone walls we cross. These walls are beautifully made, the individual stones set vertically. On the left, the land, edged with orange trefoil and pink sea thrift in summer, drops ten feet to the sea shore; on the right, it climbs a steep slope overgrown with flowering heather, gorse, briars, African grasses, and small pines.

Stonechats, pretty little birds localised in such habitat, are common here. The males, with black heads and white collars, use briars as singing posts, and are easy to see. Choughs, red-legged, red-beaked crows absent or very rare elsewhere in the British and Irish isles, may sometimes be seen, tumbling acrobatically in small flocks. Sand martins make nests in burrows dug into the low cliffs, and kestrels hover over the rough grass. Viviparous lizards are localised here, over a half mile or so of coastal land. Absent or very rare elsewhere, they may be seen basking on rocks or walls on very warm summer days.

Rock platforms and small coves edge the sea. The Dutch owner of a home on the road above has installed well-made steps by which the public may reach a small beach. Nearest the land, the rocks are covered with brilliant coloured lichens, further down, with myriad acorn barnacles and tiny seed mussels. The sea pools are crystal clear, full of sea anemones, urchins, crustaceans, crabs, small fish, pink corraline weed, sea oak and carragheen moss. Locals fish off these rocks when the mackerel shoals come in at the end of summer. The mackerel, in feeding frenzy, drive sprats before them so that rocks and sand may be silvered with whitebait, throwing themselves out of the sea to escape.

Viviparous lizard basking at Harbour View

(6) We reach the boat slip. If the tide is well out, we can now walk along the hard packed sand, back to our starting point at Flaxfort Strand. Otherwise, by the kindness of the land owner, we continue along the coast path until we reach the road, and walk half a mile along it to the car park. The beach walk is the more interesting. If it is springtime, breeding colonies of shannies, a small, amusing fish native to the wave platforms, may be found under flat rocks a long distance from the sea. They remain moist through a specialised mucus on the skin, enabling them to stay out of the water for hours. Pods of lemon-coloured whelk eggs will also be found, clinging to the underside of stones. The rocks should be replaced very carefully, so as not to crush the abundant life forms clinging beneath or buried in the sand.

The car park ends the walk. A mile down the road, to the right, is The Pink Elephant, a large bar and restaurant or, beyond it, a left turning to Kilbrittain village takes one to two friendly pubs. Kinsale, 'gourmet capital of Ireland', is about 7 miles further on.

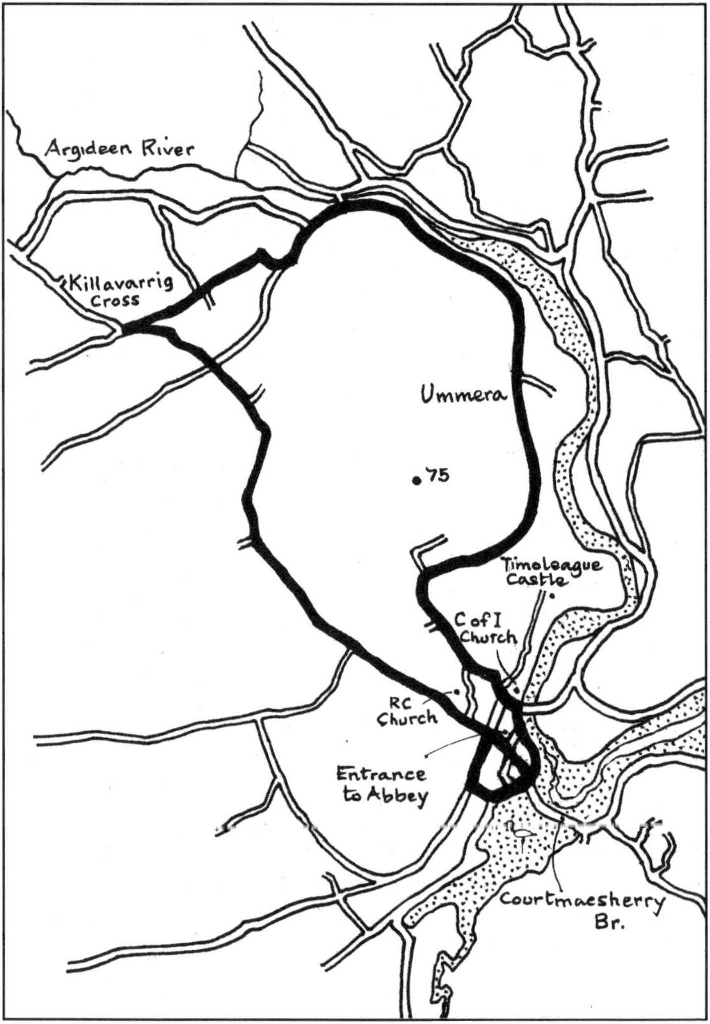

Walk No.2: Timoleague & Argideen River. 2 to 3 hours. About 4.3 miles.

Timoleague and Argideen River Walk

Historic abbey, castle, chapel and courthouse - Argideen river valley - wooded by-roads - wild flowers - views over village and bay

Locality: OS Map Sheet 86 or 89 Square 4645 Timoleague and environs, at the head of Courtmacsherry Bay. Clonakilty 6 miles, Bandon, 8, Kinsale, 13.

Description and distance: a loop walk, 4.3 miles

Walking Time: 2 to 3 hrs., including viewing the abbey. More if the Church of Ireland and the gardens of Timoleague House are taken in.

Walking conditions: Secondary roads with few cars. Two medium steep stretches.

Features: An historic Irish village, its ancient abbey, unique church and stately-home gardens. Then, out of town via wooded by-roads following the lower reaches of the River Argideen. A host of wild flowers, or forest mushrooms, in season. Panoramas over estuary and bay before arriving back at sea level and a populous bird roost, with many wader species in close proximity.

Flora and fauna: In spring and summer, wayside flowers of all varieties. In winter, fungi in the woods, and sloes and haw berries on the hedges. In winter, the bird roost attracts flocks of lapwing and golden plover as many as a thousand strong, with large numbers of curlew, oystercatcher, dunlin and redshank. Herons are common, and egrets regularly frequent the trees on the riverbank. Most local duck species may be seen.

Equipment: Everyday walking shoes.

Itinerary

(1) We begin at the car park behind Timoleague Abbey, where a gate enters the ruins. The village name is an Anglicisation of Tig Molaga, meaning the House of Molaga, having been established on the site of a 7th century monastery founded by Saint Molaga, a holy man who devoted himself to the care of plague victims and died on January 20th. AD 665, of the plague. Two booklets detailing the abbey's long history are available in the local shops, so I will simply skim the story.

The Annals of the Four Masters tell us that the foundations of the present abbey were laid by a McCarthy chieftain in 1240, the site having been a place of pilgrimage since Molaga's time. The local Norman family, the De Barras had a greater or lesser input. In 1400, the enclave was given to the Franciscan Order. Already, it had become customary for the dead of local noble families to be buried within the grounds. So many were buried there that, after four centuries, remains were disinterred and built into an ossuary wall of skulls and bones so as to make room for new burials. The poem at the gate, by an 18th century poet, records this. The tradition of burying local families around and within the abbey has been a major impediment to its restoration, as undertaken at other famous monasteries including Jerpoint, in Kilkenny, and Holy Cross, in Tipperary. There is understandable reluctance to disturb the resting places of the dead.

Timoleague Abbey was famous for its library, and was visited by the writers of the Annals of the Four Masters. There may have been a Book of Timoleague to rival The Book of Kells. There is an abiding story that, around 1840, an ancient volume was discovered by schoolboys playing in the ruins. It was thrown down from the walls and played football with, the remaining shreds providing a collation for a herd of foraging pigs.

The village was a centre of commerce before Bandon town was even founded. There are extant accounts of the market places and hostelries of the town, burgeoning with Spanish and French merchants, and the friars are known to have conducted a thriving trade in wine.

(2) Exiting the abbey via the same gate, we turn left and walk down a wide pedestrian path along the graveyard wall. After crossing the road to the near side of the Courtmacsherry bridge, we make our way along the grass verge beside the water. An imposing perspective of the abbey is gained from here,

Timoleague Abbey – western prospect

with excellent photo opportunites. Passing the picnic tables, we shortly meet the main road at the bridge spanning the River Argideen. It is worth crossing the road to lean on the parapet and look up-river. A classic view of Timoleague House and castle is presented from here. Egrets, small white storks new to Ireland, favour the riverside trees, often reflected in the placid brown waters. The castle, in ruins, stands behind the house. It was built by the de Barrys in 1214, shortly after the Norman invasion of Ireland - in fact, the Barrys arrived in Ireland before Strongbow. Over the centuries, it changed hand, often in violent circumstances, between Barrys and McCarthys, Norman and Irish overlords. A pamphlet, authored by Robert Travers, present owner of the house and lands, provides the vivid details.

In 1642, Cromwellian soldiers attacked the castle and failing to take it, burnt the abbey. They took the castle later that year. In 1820, Jonas Travers, B.L. bought the castle and 200 acres from the creditors of one "Hellgate" Barrymore, a Regency rake who had squandered the Barry fortune and died at 23. The Travers family built Timoleague House in the early 19th. century and contributed much to the reinforcing and conservation of the abbey. During the 'Troubles' of the 1920, the castle was garrisoned, and badly damaged by an explosion. It was later partly demolished when it endangered the nearby railway line - The Timoleague and Courtmacsherry Light Railway - which ran along the Argideen banks beneath its walls. The house was burnt by the IRA in the early 1920's, but was rebuilt in 1923 using the same stones.

(3) Facing upriver, we turn left and follow the church wall which rounds a corner to the right. In June, this wall is covered in the purple blooms of valerian. The Church of Ireland chapel, within the walls, is unique. The grounds are lovely, with mature yews and a small, well kept graveyard. But it is the interior which brings the surprise. Tiled in exotic mosaic, the south wall resembles more a corner of the Taj Mahal than an Irish country chapel interior. A plaque records that the work was effected at the expense of the Maharajah of Gwalior, as a memorial to his physician, Lieut. Col. Crofts of the Indian Medical Service, who saved his son's life. Croft's parish church was Timoleague. Other fine mosaics, by Minton of London, also grace this lovely chapel, many of them memorials to members of the Travers family. Leaving the church, we turn right and immediately arrive at the gates of Timoleague House, the fine gardens of which are open to the public on most days from June to August. For details, tel. 023 46116.

Our route passes the gates, and sets off out of the village, passing the imposing Catholic Church on the left. This, built on a site given by the Travers family, was completed in1912, and has a fine window on the west side, added in 1931, the work of an Irish master of stained glass, Harry Clark. The ancient Timoleague Chalice, with which the last abbey friars fled during Penal times, was found in a house on Cape Clear Island in 1856, and is now once again in the keeping of the parish.

Little Egret, Argideen estuary

The large house on the left is the Glebe House, which was the Church of Ireland vicar's residence. On the right, the high stone walls of Timoleague House estate follow the road Old stone walls in south west Ireland are vertical gardens, supporting a wide and fecund growth of plants. Here, as elsewhere, we will find navelworth with bell-like flowers shooting to 50cm. tall, wall rue and delicate maiden hair, herb robert, with pink flowers, bright purple violets, white stitchworth, and even foxgloves, which may be 2m. tall, sometimes gain a hold.

Meanwhile, depending on the time of year, the verges may be blue with bluebells, white with ransomes, creamy with primroses or golden with buttercups. The 'long acres' of the Irish roadsides are gardens of delight and it is well worth carrying a pocket guide to identify all one will find.

Stands of beeches line the estate walls, and then a stand of conifers. Below,

Inkcaps and clitocybe on roadside

the Argideen estuary may be glimpsed and Courtmacsherry Bay with, above it, the heights of Barreragh, another walk outlined in this book. The wall is now gapped; obviously, its erstwhile stolid splendour harks back to a time when Irish labour was cheap and such estates could be maintained.

(4) We are walking on the high land over the western bank of the Argideen. The woodland along the roadside provides cover for many birds. Warblers may be heard in spring and summer, along with the rusty-hinge squeaks of young long-eared owls and the raucous cackling of pheasants, when disturbed. The mossy banks of the woods are carpeted with golden celandine. In winter, when the trees are bare, foraging bands of long tailed tits are a regular feature, and goldcrests can be heard - and seen - in the canopy of pines. Breaks in the trees provide views over the river, on the shaded waters of which swim many swans. A sparrowhawk occupies an old pigeon nest near the gateway to Ummera House.

Ummera House nowadays produces exclusive smoked wild salmon. The house is set in fine pastures, with tree lined drive typical of the 'planter's house' of the 18th century. It commands views of the river, and fishing rights along its frontage. Below a modern cottage on the left, we can see excellent examples of Irish stone wall construction, with the stones set vertically, rather than horizontally.

Beyond Ummera, a small tributary crosses beneath the road, lined with alder and salix (sally trees). When in decent spate, it 'babbles', as all brooks should and, in the rural peace, it is worth pausing to listen to, perhaps leaning on the small, stone bridge.

The grass courts and pavilion of the Arigideen Vale Lawn Tennis and Croquet Club are on the left. This was, of course, initially a venue for the local Protestant ascendancy and reminds one of long lady's skirts, headbands, heavy rackets and honey for tea. The first local Open Tennis Tournament took place in 1892.

We pass an unfortunate chicken unit on the right. Soon, marsh marigolds and flag irises carpet the wet ground by the river below us. After tunnels of trees and thick leaf mould where wood anemones grow in spring and tasty wood blewitts and parasol mushrooms in winter, we come to Inchy Bridge. The Argideen has long been one of Munster's most famous sea trout and salmonid rivers. Here, the best of intentions, volunteer labour and a Leader grant has created wheelchair access to allow the disabled to fish immediately in front of the picturesque bridge. At the moment, the concrete structure and galvanised handrails totally eclipse the beauty of the arches but will, one hopes, in time become overgrown and compatible with the scene. Over this pool, in summer, bats flit, including Daubenton's, the water bat, and fishermen have had them take their dry fly. Kingfishers are resident, and dippers, the small bird that walks beneath the water and hunts between the riverbed stones.

(5) We do not cross the bridge, but continue straight ahead to the building of Barryroe Coop and a signpost for Ballinascarthy and Clonakilty. We see, 100 metres ahead, fishing lodges sensitively restored from ancient stone barns by Tim Severin, explorer and author of "The Brendan Voyage". But we bear left, past a house with many-headed cordylline palms. Shortly, a road goes off to our left; we can take this and shorten our walk by, perhaps, a half mile. But, continuing to the right, we pass another house with hydra-headed palms and a plain, straight country road to Killavarrig Cross Roads. Here, we take the left turning, doubling back, up the hill. The climb is steep but, happily, short, and as we ascend we get wonderful panoramic views of the country to the west and north of us, large, rich fields, scrubby woodlands, and hill tops with heather and gorse.

We pass through a crossroads - the road plunging down to the left is the access from the shorter route, mentioned earlier. Now, on these high lands, we can see for miles. Wild strawberries are common on the roadside ditches. At a break of gorse, and a gurgling stream, a 'dog leg' turning takes us up another short steep climb. "No fox hunting", requests a notice on a gate. 'Foot-bagels' is a common West Cork pastime but, happily, the beagles almost never catch a fox and the fox population of Ireland is robust.

Hedges and ditches in bloom

On this road, there are three climbs between Killavarrig and the 'summit' at Ardmore, but there are breaks between them, and none are very long or steep. At Ardmore, there is a farm with extensive outbuildings, and then we set off downhill towards Timoleague. The road is straight and, immediately, we have a magnificent view of Courtmacsherry Bay, Courtmacsherry itself to the west, with Wood Point beyond, and Harbour View on the eastern side. It is a classic vista of a broad, winding estuary, with salients of land abutting into the old river's flow. When the tide is out, hundreds of acres of mudflats are exposed, their myriad invertebrate life supporting the 20,000 or more birds that migrate to here each winter. With each tide, billions of gallons of water sweep in but the rise is such that, but for the deeper channels, a tall person could almost walk from one side of the bay to the other. The tide comes in quickly over the rippled sand; it is quite extraordinary how fast it moves.

Steeply descending, we pass bungalows, and verges where orange montbretia, a garden escapee now wild in Ireland, grows in profusion, and lords-and-ladies, those unusual lily-like plants.
First, we see the spire of the Catholic Church, then a gable of the Abbey, then the Argideen, and Timoleague House and the Castle. The Abbey layout is clearly seen from here, the tower rising at the centre, the chapels and library, the graveyard to one side. The painted houses of Timoleague appear, shocking pink, papal purple, tropical azure and apple green- the Irish are, indeed, fearless with paint! A copse of trees beyond the bridge across the bay is a flourishing rookery and anyone who wishes to be impressed by the cohesion of rooks need only watch them in their thousands spill out of this wood at twilight to cross the bay and back in raucous curtains, darkening the darkening sky.

Magpie and fox cub, springtime

Reaching the village, at the crossroads at its centre, we turn right. On the left is an imposing building, with five arches. Built in about 1696, it initially served as a market house on the ground floor, and an Assizes Court above. Bought and restored from semi-dereliction by this writer and his wife, it is now a school where students come from all over the globe to learn the English language. In 1821, riots by the Catholic Irish against demands to pay tithes to Protestant clergy led to a murder for which local men were to be arraigned. Daniel O'Connell, "The Liberator", arrived unexpectedly to defend them, whether successfully or not is not known. A brass plaque commemorates his visit.

At the corner, we turn left and pass the Filling Station. If it is evening and low tide, and anytime between October and April, the slob in front of the metal bridge is likely to be carpeted in birds. Huge flocks of lapwing and golden plover rise and fly in intricate formations again and again before settling down. Redshanks and curlew wing in to roost, and tiny dunlin flash and turn in dazzling display. Ducks and swans drift quietly in the shallow pools.

Walking along the water, with the playing field on the left, we reach the north end of the bridge. Opposite, a closed walkway leads, through bollards, to the Abbey entrance, and we are back where we began.

Two hundred yards away, at the crossroads in the village centre are many hostelries. Timoleague has been famous down the ages for its its hospitality. Where better to enjoy a post-walk repast or drink?

Barreragh & Abbeymahon Walk

The west end of Courtmacsherry village - Siberia - woods of Earl of Shannon estate - elevated views of Courtmacsherry Bay with Timoleague and Timoleague Abbey - Abbeymahon Monastery ruins - wading bird roost.

Locality: OS Sheet 87 Square 5042. Courtmacsherry, the village and hinterland to the south west. Bandon 9 miles, Clonakilty 8, Timoleague 2. We climb gently from sea level to 125 metres and then descend again to the bay shore.

Description and distance: A loop walk, 4.5 miles, beginning and ending in the village, climbing gently from sea level to 125 metres and then descending to the bay shore.

Walking Time: 2 hrs.

Walking conditions: Quiet back roads with few, if any, cars. Village pavements and woodland path. A short section of secondary road, with occasional cars. One fairly long, but gentle, incline.

Features: Historic Courtmacsherry village, and pier. Old woodland. A panoramic vista of Courtmacsherry Bay. Remnants of the famous Timoleague-Courtmacsherry Light Railway. A roadside memorial to a West Cork Brigade volunteer killed in battle with British forces in 1921. The ruins of an ancient Cistercian monastery. An important high tide roost for wading birds.

Flora and fauna: Roadside flora. Birds of the uplands, bay shores and bay. For migrants, Courtmacsherry Bay is the most important numerically of all West Cork estuaries. Up to 20,000 waders and sea birds of 24 species are present during winter months. The estuary is ranked an internationally important site for black tailed godwits, and hosts nationally important numbers of golden plover, dunlin, lapwing, curlew, redshank, shelduck, merganser and cormorant.

Equipment: Comfortable walking shoes.

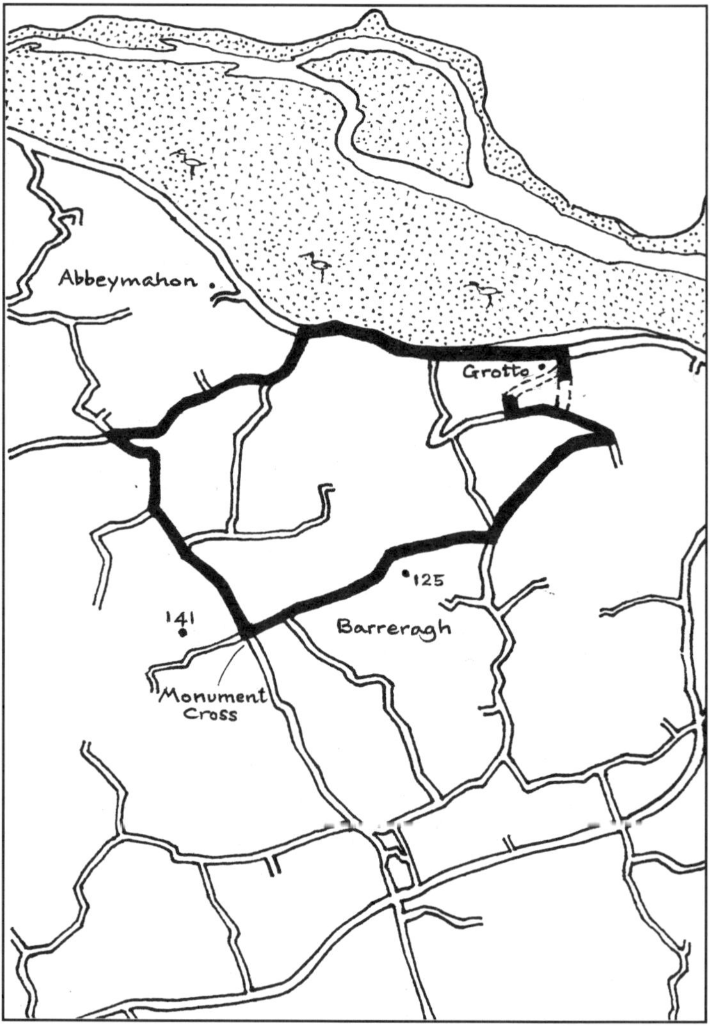

Walk No.3: Barreragh and Abbeymahon. 2 hours. About 4.5 miles.

Itinerary

(1) Courtmacsherry is a linear village, population 200 in winter, with gaily painted houses lining the single pavement, and the bay on the opposite side of the road. It is sheltered by old woods, behind.

The name derives from Cuirt Mhic Sheafraidh, the court of the son of Geoffrey, Geoffrey being a name adopted by the Norman Hodnett family when they "became more Irish than the Irish themselves". The village has long been a small resort, and many Cork business families have had holiday homes here for generations. A contemporary account tells us that, in the early19th century, "several well-appointed houses" (Hamilton's Row and Terrace) made the village "one of the most fashionable bathing places on the south coast".

We begin our walk at the pier. Sea angling boats operate from here all summer, taking anglers out to fish the numerous local ship wrecks or to catch sharks, which are tagged and returned to the sea. A few small fishing boats also operate. While public subscription and EU funds raised finance to extend the pier and provide yachting facilities in 1997, there has been little funding available to local fishermen since the 1960's government trade-offs of fishing rights in exchange for farming subsidies. This is since regretted as EU partners harvest Ireland's natural fishing grounds. The lack of support for the Irish fishing industry is exemplified in the sorry state of the boats in which local men struggle to make a living. In the 19th century, several schooners were locally owned, and yawls were built each year at the local boatyard. Up to recently, when salmon drift netting was still viable, a dozen boats worked the estuary, while sand barges and colliers unloaded their cargoes at the busy pier.

The most impressive craft to be seen in the channel today is the Courtmacsherry lifeboat. It is notable that, from the population of 200, the hamlet still provides enough brave volunteers to man the lifeboat whatever the weather. The first lifeboat in Ireland was at Courtmacsherry and Courtmacsherry men have risked their lives for others since 1825. Rowing six miles from Barry's Point, they were the first lifeboat to reach the Lusitania, sunk by a U boat off the Old Head of Kinsale on 7th of May, 1915, with a loss of 1,200 lives. The RNLI is a British institution but continued its good work in Ireland after Independence.

Above the village may be seen the Old Coast Guard Station. The largest fortified Station in Ireland - the gun ports may still be seen - it was built about 1869 and torched by the rebel Irish in 1922 when, it was said, "the Irish burnt everything British except their coal". The arsonists, trying to buy a large quantity of kerosene at the local Post Office-cum-shop, were refused by the shop keeper until a pistol was laid on the counter. The building was extensively renovated in 1972 and converted to holiday apartments.

Wood Point and Old Head of Kinsale

Leaving the pier, we pass the wooden Railway Station, now a private dwelling. Here, in former years, happy crowds arrived each summer Sunday on excursion trains from Cork. One train alone, on August Bank Holiday, 1953, brought 600 day trippers. From September to January, the trains drew sugar beet from the rich farmlands of Timoleague and Barryroe. The railway was closed in 1961, and is still bemoaned as a great loss.

As we walk, we see Burren Pier across the bay, here only a half mile wide. The grassy right hand verge follows the track of the old railway along the bay to Timoleague. A large, painted map by the roadside illustrates the Seven Heads and the coast from Wood Point to Dunworley. On it, we can trace the route we will be taking, south to the uplands, and circling back down to Abbeymahon and the sea. The overlordship of the Norman De Barras (Barrys) is evident in the place names - Barryroe, Barry's Point, Travarra, etc. Also illustrated are the positions of shipwrecks, including the Lusitania, and the positions of Signal Towers along the coast. There is a pleasant picnic table in front of the map, and the large anchor of the Cardiff Hall, sunk, with all hands, off the Seven Heads, 1925. (see Seven Heads Walk) is displayed close by.

The Community Hall is on the right, and, on the left, a grotto of the Virgin Mary, followed by a terrace of gaily painted council houses. This end of Courtmacsherry is called, even on the maps, "Siberia", although the weather is generally as mild as elsewhere in this sheltered Gulf Stream village. The presence of palms in the park and gardens surely refutes this dire slur and evidences Courtmacsherry's rightful Riviera reputation!

(2) We turn sharp left just before the Grotto. A green path can be seen leading to the woods above. On summer evenings, an amazing number of pipistrelle bats issues from the eaves at the back of one of the nearby modern houses, a veritable river of bats flowing into the darkening air. Once, we tried to count them, but gave up at 805.

The green pathway winds to the right, making the climb more gentle, and ascends between ivyied stone walls to the woodland above. We begin to get elevated views of the bay, a foretaste of the magnificent panoramas to come. These woods are part of the old Earl of Shannon estate, recorded as sheltering the village from "the sea-winds" in Smith's History of Cork (1750). The Earl of Shannon acquired the lands about that time, and planted further woods at the harbour mouth. There are many exotics, including an ancient cork oak in front of the hotel, the earls' one-time summer residence. These woods lend Courtmacsherry its classic 'chocolate box' beauty, mirror-still water reflecting multicoloured boats and houses, and stately woods behind.

The track climbs the wooded slope. As we reach the last trees, we turn right off the main track (which continues to a tarred road after 200 metres) and follow a narrow woodland path. The path runs due west, winding through the trees. Below, the backs of the village houses, and glimpses of the bay, limited or extensive depending on the foliage and the time of year.

The Memorial Cross, War of Independence, 1921

The path ends at steps set into a stone wall, and we walk twenty metres along a raised ditch to join a narrow, gently ascending tarred road. We turn left to join it. In winter, flocks of gulls, curlews and black and white oystercatchers forage on the fields on either side. We are briefly walking east now. Ahead, we see the wide

The ruins at Abbeymahon, with stonechat

strip of woodland that backs the village and runs down the western arm of the bay to Wood Point. Beyond, across the bay mouth, we see Coolmain Strand and Coolmain Castle, owned by the Walt Disney family. Directly opposite us, across the estuary, is the Burren House, a fine Georgian residence. There are many such 'planter's houses' between here and Bandon, nine miles away. Bandon was an English stronghold during the Plantation of Munster and afterwards. The dispossessed Catholic Irish were disbarred from entering the walled town for 200 years. Fine trees invariably grace the avenues of the landlords' houses. As the poet Austin Clark noted, "The house of the planter is surrounded by trees."

As we turn a sharp corner and head west again, we see another such house across the bay, Lisheen, one of the old houses of the Scott family, who still own much of the land around it. The slope continues, pleasantly energetic. The roadside vegetation is hart's-tongue, hard fern and navelwort, with occasional blackthorns and fuschias looking rather 'shook' with the wind. We pass a new house, called "Shalom" and arrive at a 'staggered' cross roads. The first right turn plunges steeply back towards the bay. We take the second right, still climbing gently.

We are soon at Barreragh or Barr Aerach, ("Airy Top"), high above the world, a bracing spot with the best views for miles. Roadside gorse and whitethorn bloom in season. Far below and to the left is the inner bay, with the many coloured houses of Timoleague village climbing the hill, and the ruins of13th century Timoleague Abbey by the water. Gleaming wetlands, where flocks of wading birds roost, lie beside the estuary of the River Argideen. Beyond Timoleague, the hills of West Cork stretch to the horizon.

Turning 180°, we see, six miles off, the wide mouth of the bay, mile-long Garretstown Strand, the long arm of the Old Head of Kinsale, its lighthouse, and the open Atlantic. To the south east, across the peninsula, Barry's Point is visible, and it is possible to make out the old Life Boat Station, half way along the headland, from whence the boat that reached the Lusitania was launched.

(3) At the next cross road, an iron cross stands on a plinth painted green, white and gold, surrounded by a wrought iron railing, slightly out of true. This is a memorial cross for an IRA volunteer who died in a skirmish with British forces during the War of Independence. A copper plaque, inscribed in lovely Gaelic script, records that at this spot Paid O Donnabain, aged 21, a volunteer in the 3rd Brigade of the Cork IRA, gave his life for Ireland on January 16th, 1921. It is a lonely place, where a single gnarled tree stands behind the cross, and the four winds blow.

We turn right now, and start downhill towards the bay. Below us, the ruined gable of the old church of Abbeymahon can be seen between the trees. The bohreen is sheltered by high ditches, and the student of botany will enjoy the wealth of wild plants growing amongst the gorse and the ferns. The sorrel is particularly good to eat, sharp and sour on the palate.

(4) After the road levels, we come to a cross where we turn right, staying on this road until we reach the shore at Ballynamona Cross, and go left two hundred yards to visit the ruins at Abbeymahon.

As an alternative, we may continue straight ahead, along an unsurfaced lane, adding a mile distance to the walk. In winter, the first section, running between farmyards, is extremely muddy, but a right turn at the next T-junction takes us quickly along a paved bohreen to a pleasant 'green road' beneath beeches and thence downhill to the bay shore. In this case, we turn right and immediately come upon the ruins at Abbeymahon.

Sometime before 1272, Cistercian monks moved from their first house at Aghmanister, near Timoleague, to Abbeymahon where they remained until the monastery was suppressed in 1537. The priests and lay brothers farmed land in all the surrounding parishes and the Rev. James Coombes, in his booklet "Timoleague and Barryroe", wonders if their work might have initiated the "sturdy tradition of husbandry" for which Barryroe farmers are noted. The surviving gable of an ancient keep attached to the monastery stands on private land nearby.

Turning to walk the half mile back to Courtmacsherry, we immediately pass a stand of low reeds just off shore. Between October and March, four varieties of duck may be seen feeding here. Most obvious are the large, elegant shelduck. Chestnut, black and white, they hoover the mud with their brilliant red beaks for small crustaceans. After nesting in rabbit burrows, in August the parent birds leave the ducklings in a creche, supervised by selected adults, while the bulk of the flock flies to Heligoland, in the German Bight, to moult. They return two months later and reclaim their offspring. Present here, also, are tiny teal, with swept-back Chinese eyes and plumage that gleams like lacquer when it catches the light. Widgeon, with ruddy heads and white wing bars, and glossy-headed mallard also feed amongst the reeds.

Shelduck, courting

Fifty yards after Ballynamona Cross, we pass Peter's Point, a small, low promontory inside the sea wall. This seemingly insignificant outcrop is of immense importance as a high tide roost for waders and literally hundreds of tiny dunlin, ringed plover, godwits, redshank, greenshank, lapwing, whim-

Wood mouse with barley

brel, and curlew crowd together on the margins when the tide is high. We pass quietly; the birds ignore cars but are easily disturbed by walkers. Hereabouts, a peregrine falcon is regularly seen raising the flocks, or perched on the roadside fence posts after feeding. When the flocks rise, they fly in synchronised zig-zags, like chequered tablecloths shook out against the sky. The kaleidoscope effect is a defence against the falcon.

Back, then, along the shore side verge to the village. A scheme is in place to turn the track of the old railway into a walking path, and this may be accomplished by 1999. In any case, it is a lovely walk along the bay, and it is only a short distance before we reach the pavement just after the 30mph signs. To the right, is the Catholic church and a row of brightly painted houses facing the children's playground, where cordyline palm trees grow.

There are three pubs in the village. From personal experience, I know that each assures a warm welcome to the walker, pleasant terraces in summer, a roaring fire in winter, hot and cold drinks, conversation and even song. Full meals may be had at the hotel, a half mile further. There are pleasant coves along the headland, from which to swim.

Courtmacsherry Walk

The east end of Courtmacsherry village - old woodland paths - coves and sea cliffs - the unique cottages of Meelmaan - a long storm beach

Locality: OS Map Sheet 87 Square 5242, Courtmacsherry and Broad Strand. Clonakilty 8 miles, Bandon 9, Kinsale, 15.

Description and Distance: 3 loop walks (A) 4 miles (B) 5 miles (C) 6 miles

Walking Time: between 2 and 3 hrs, depending on option

Walking conditions: woodland paths, open fields and cliff path, bohreens, beach, secondary road with occasional cars. No steep inclines.

Features: Fresh air and away-from-it-all feeling. Diverse woodland. Open fields overlooking the broad Atlantic. A hamlet of unique cottages. A magnificent beach, usually deserted. Home via country roads to where we began.

Flora and fauna: In Spring, the woodland floor is, literally, carpeted with bluebells, wood anemones and ramsons. The trees are diverse species. Ravens, hooded crows and parties of red-beaked, red-legged, glossy-black choughs are often seen foraging in the cliff fields. Boxing hares are seen in spring. Seals frequent the coves and swim close in to the beach at Broad Strand Bay.

In November, sprat shoals get trapped in Broad Strand or Coolbawn (Option C) just beyond. For a few days, one of the finest wild-life spectaculars in Ireland ensues, with thousands of sea birds feeding, including big, white gannets diving in formation, large rafts of guillemots, razorbills and mergansers, and thousands of kittiwakes. As many as twenty seals wallow only a stone's throw from the shore.

Equipment: Comfortable walking shoes.

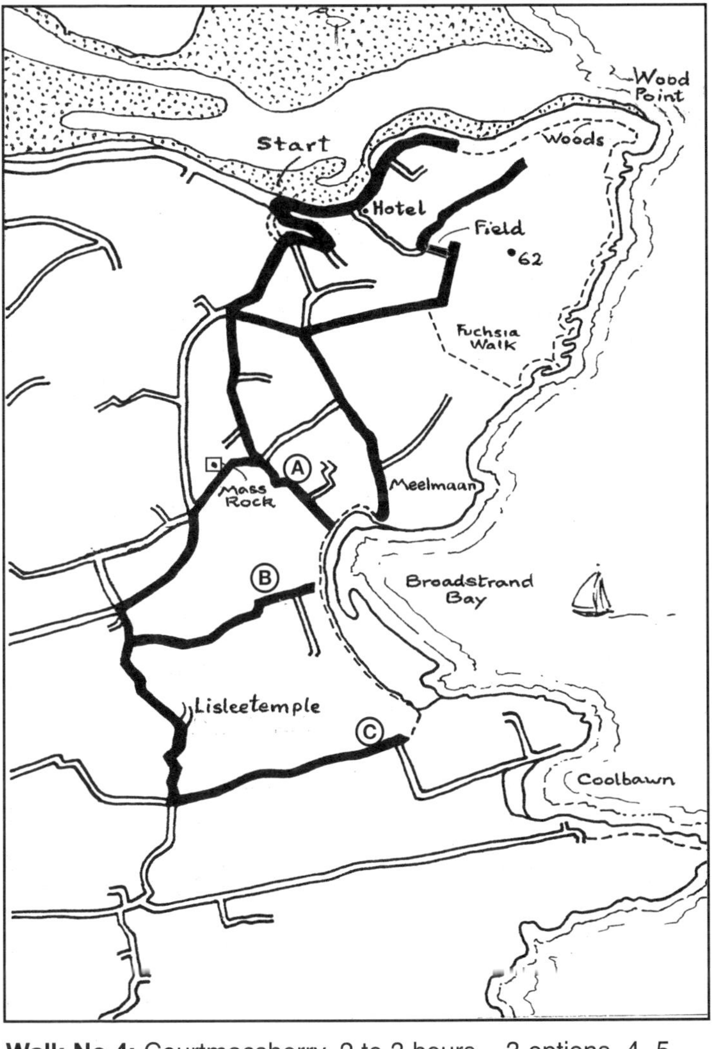

Walk No.4: Courtmacsherry. 2 to 3 hours – 3 options, 4, 5, or 6 miles.

Itinerary

(1) We set off from the small St John the Evangelist Church of Ireland at the east end of pretty Courtmacsherry village. Sunday services are held in July and August. The village has a number of summer homes handed down through generations of prominent Cork C of I families.

Cormorant on Broad Strand, with Quarry Point in background

Ignoring the turn up the hill to the right, we walk along the sea, with the bay on our left. A few hundred yards along, we pass the remains of the old pier, and the old stone building of Seaview Court. A road leads right just before the hotel gates; we ignore it, and pass in front of the hotel, originally the summer residence of The Earls of Shannon, whose year round quarters were at Kincragie, a once lovely house now a mouldering ruin in the woods above. An ancient cork oak tree grows in the centre of the hotel lawn, gnarled and exotic. Ti trees, (Cordyline Australis), or "palms" as they are locally known, flourish in the mild Gulf Stream climate of West Cork, and especially well here by the sea where there is rarely frost. The examples at the hotel are many headed, indicating that they have died back, possibly through snow - a few days of which occurs, on average, every three years - and re-sprouted. Native of Asia and Pacific islands, they lend a tropical air to the village gardens.

In front of the hotel is a sandy beach and a picnic area. When the tide is out, the foreshore is dotted with the coiled casts of lugworm, bait for dabs or bass. Grey herons often stand vigil and, in winter, parties of curlew, godwit, redshank, oystercatcher and turnstones patrol the mud nearer the channel. Great northern divers are regular in winter, fishing very close in-shore along with mergansers - colourful sawbill ducks - and cormorants. In summer, family parties of terns fly over the bay, the young calling to their parents for food. They are exciting to watch as they dive onto the shoals of whitebait, raising small plumes of spray. An otter frequents this shore, and has been known to fish along the sea wall in the middle of the day.

The view of the village behind us is very fine, with the coloured houses, the boats and the pier. This is a good spot for sunset photographs, with red skies over the village as the sun sinks beyond it to the west.

(2) As we reach the solitary house at the extreme east end of the beach, we turn up a lane way to the right, flanked on the right side by bungalows. This takes us to The Meadow which, at the time of writing, is still a large, open field. Paths lead across it. Do not go too near the cliff edge, as it is eroded. Below, lies the beach which extends in a long, narrow strip at low tide. The edge of the woods and the water are reminiscent of a Canadian lake shore.

We enter the woods, and find a broad path immediately. These woods are old and we see mighty beeches lying where they fell. In spring, the forest floor is carpeted in bluebells, which climb the slope to the right in a haze of purple. White ransoms, smelling of garlic, and delicate wood anemones, which close in the evening, are other flowers of the woods. There are a variety of mushrooms in autumn, including blewits, parasols and russula, and beechmast and hazel nuts. Some locals claim to have seen red squirrels in the canopy but, if there, they are rarely seen. Long eared owls nest in a tree hollow.

Meelmaan village, over Broad Strand

The pathway is good and this walk, a local section of the Seven Heads Walk, is popular at any time of the year. In summer, when the trees are verdant and ivy glistens in the sun, shafts of light filter through the canopy and light up the path. Many of the trees are gnarled and twisted, ivy or moss covered, with polypody ferns growing along the high branches, and giant male ferns growing beneath. The waxy, shiny leaves of hart's tongue ferns - shaped like the tongue of a deer - may be up to three feet long. The proliferation and size of the ferns and the mossy, fern-grown trees, with honeysuckle creeper hanging from the branches, gives these temperate woods an Amazonian air. Exotic orange montbretia - a garden escapee now widespread in south-west Ireland - flowers along the paths in summer.

To the left of the path, are small coves, some sandy and very pleasant for swimming. Anglers fish for bass off the rocks, and the rock pools are full of small shannies and blennies, colourful sea anemones, prawns and crabs. The rocks are covered in acorn barnacles, with clumps of seed mussels, many

A rock pool teeming with life

limpets, whelks and winkles. Across the water are Harbour View beach, Coolmaine beach, the Disney castle and the shadowed coves and caves along Coolmaine Point.

We pass the Wishing Well, so called. There is a badger sett to the left of it, and a well-worn badger run. The path we follow is now partly stone paved - these woods, in the 19th century, were commercially managed by the Earl of Shannon estate. The old oaks form tunnels over it, and we pass small stands of birch and hazel.

(3) About a mile from where we began, we emerge from the trees onto a magnificent view. This is Wood Point - The Point of the Wood, as the name persists locally - the southern mouth of Courtmacsherry Bay. Ahead is the broad Atlantic, with Barry's Point to the south and the Old Head of Kinsale, and lighthouse, to the east. There is a beacon here, marking the harbour entrance, and a buoy off shore. White water breaks on the rocks below, and kelp gleams on the surface when the tide is low. A seal's head may be sometimes seen amongst the kelp; grey seals are curious, and are as interested in us as we are in them.

The path leads along the cliff top, below a wire fence that skirts the field where horses often graze and mushrooms sometimes grow. The route meanders between low gorse, and here the intrepid may descend (not recommended) to The Frying Pan, a rocky cove of deep water, azure and crystal-clear beneath summer skies, where the local youth swim and romance. The cliff wall is flat slabs of rock facing the sun, inclined at an angle of 60° , and wonderful to lie against for sun-bathing. There are rocks to dive from, and small rocky islands to swim to. It is an idyllic spot on a summer day.

From these rocks, also, locals and visitors fish for mackerel on summer evenings, when the shoals come in-shore. The big, cruciform white gannets, with black wing tips, plummet into the sea amongst them, raising spouts of spray. Basking sharks, up to thirty foot long, may occasionally be seen, lazily cruising on the surface, their large triangular fin out of the water, their huge mouths agape. There can be few finer places to sit on the cliffs and watch as the sun, setting behind one, lights up the sea, the distant white beaches of Garretstown and the Old Head of Kinsale.

Now, at Coomalacha, also called the Frying Pan, there is a raven's nest on an inaccessible ledge on the cliff side. The sea swills or lashes in below, depending on the weather. The ravens - large black crows, with heavy beaks - are generally close by, summer or winter. It is a lonely spot, but time honoured by ravens. The nest base, although wind-torn each winter, is tidied up in January and built on. Ravens are our earliest nesting birds. They mate for life, and when a partner dies, a young bird immediately takes up its place, so that there is a continuum of ravens at the same site, never breaking the tenancy or the genetic chain. This raven family may have been there for a millennium. They are storied birds, in every mythology. Celtic legend credits them with prediction. Norse battle standards bore an image of the raven, and those who marched behind it must have been familiar with the bird, scavenging the dead.

We reach the first field division, just beyond the raven's cove - we are on private property, by kind permission of the owner - and can look down at rocks where the local youth sunbathe and swim in summer, an idyllic spot with deep, clear water and south-facing rocks faces tilted perfectly towards the sun. A small stream, with a break of reeds below it, makes the ground wet here in winter.

We pass along the bottoms of the cliff-top fields. The stiles were created by the landowners — as in the woods, we are on private property, by kind permission of the owners. We pass through a small copse of conifers. Parasol mushrooms grow very well here, appearing when the weather suits them between August and November. A few fields further on, we reach a bridge made of railways sleepers fording a small stream and the southern end of the Fuchsia Walk, as it is known.

(4) From here to the meadow overlooking Broad Strand, the old path along the cliff top is often difficult, the land ploughed almost to the edge. To walk up the Fuchsia Walk and approach Broad Strand by country lanes may be the best option. It is a pleasant green track between fuchsia hedges and blackthorns, created in the nineteenth century as a private route by which the ladies in the Earl of Shannon's household might reach the beach at File na Bro, just beyond the small stream; erosion has now made it almost inaccessible. Badgers may sometimes be seen, at dusk, on the Fuchsia Walk; there is a busy sett a few hundred yards along. When we reach the 'top', we find three stone steps, taking us out onto a road.

(5) Here, we turn left. In 2004, a new estate was built on the right and now, as we near the cross-roads, we are briefly in suburbia, with pavements and street lights. At the cross-roads, we turn left. Courtmacsherry Bay is now directly behind us and we are walking almost due south.

This elevated road affords panoramic views all the way to the Old Head. With binoculars, one can make out Holeopen Bay, with a cave beneath the headland through which, at low water, a small boat may pass to the other side. We pass the right turning at Hilltop House, and continue straight ahead. The road now descends to a quaint and quite unique hamlet of a few houses and ruins. This is Meelmaan, overlooking the big storm beach of Broad Strand, and Horse Rock, to the east.

Lissleetemple Church

Here, until just a few years ago, chickens might be seen scratching in the dust, and a cat or dog found lying in the middle of the thoroughfare of a summer day. Some of the old houses have been renovated or knocked, and new houses built. Meelmaan has the unique distinction of a number of cottages with roof ridges which parallel the steep downward slope of the road, so that the gable at the top end is some five feet higher than that at the bottom. It has been suggested that if children had their bedrooms in the attics, they would move from the lower end to the higher end as they grew. It seems that the same unsung artisan was the author of most of the village houses, and ruins showing his original feature also remain. One hopes that those refurbishing the latter for holiday homes will retain this priceless feature of design.

The road ends at the bottom of the village. In times past, the overgrown track ahead continued, crossing the sands below and joining a similarly overgrown track visible at the other end of the long beach. Below the last village house on the right, we take a narrow, almost concealed path between tall fuchsia hedges - a palm tree in the garden overlooks it - and pass through the stone wicket at the end. We cross a field - by the good graces of its owner - and make for the lower corner. Here, our handsome Irish hooded crows are often seen, unavailable for viewing in England, where they are replaced by the carrion crow. They are very successful; I have seen them driving a peregrine falcon off its kill. At the bottom, we negotiate a paling fence, and descend a few feet to the car park.

(6) The open crescent of Broad Strand now lies before us. Lit by southern or western light, it glitters magically at low tide and is usually deserted. From here, there is a fine panorama of the coast from Barry's Point to the Old Head. We now have three options;
whichever option we chose, the long beach itself is worth the walk. Occasionally orphan seals come ashore and the near sea teems with life when the sprat shoals come in, in late summer and November. Then, big rafts of guillemot, razorbill, cormorant, shag and merganser ride the swells just beyond the surf. The sky above is full of screaming, diving kittiwakes and gannets. Large seals roll and romance in the waves. In summer, record bass are caught from the beach.

Three Options for the route back to Courtmacsherry: A, B and C.

All three routes off Broad Strand bring us out on the Barryroe-Courtmacsherry road where, turning right, leading back to Courtmac village.

For Option A, we exit the beach via the road at the car park. Reaching the four-cross-roads, we go straight across. A brief diversion up the road to the left takes us to a Mass Rock, where fugitive priests said illicit mass in Penal times. Returning to the cross roads, we continue due north, as first indicated, to a T-junction. On this larger road, we take a right turn to Courtmacsherry, as signposted.

For Option B, we exit the beach via the road at the centre. At the T-junction, we turn right and, 100 yards along, right again on the main road back to Courtmacsherry. At the next cross, we turn right, which takes us past the Mass Rock above mentioned, and down to the four cross roads. There, the left turn takes us back to the main road and the signposted right turn to Courtmacsherry. This route has the advantage of passing the Mass Rock and keeping us off the main road.

For Option C, we exit via the far (i.e. southern) end of the beach. Steps take us via the track of the old road that crossed the beach. We emerge onto a tarred road on a corner, and turn right, continuing until we reach the first four-cross-roads, where we turn right again. We pass ruined Lislee Temple and old graveyard; this Protestant church was built on the site of a pre-Reformation chapel. Ignoring the first turn to the right, we ascend to a four-cross-roads and turn right on the main road to Courtmacsherry. At the next cross, we turn right down the Mass Rock road, and continue as outlined in Option B.

Lesser Black Backed Gull, Courtmacsherry

As we walk downhill towards the village, we see a large white sign on the left announcing "Courtmacsherry-Cuirt Mhic Sheafraidh" (the court of the son of Geoffrey - see Barreragh Walk). Immediately beside it is a small concrete hut and a pleasant woodland right-of-way leading to the road below. The path is steep, and only the sure-footed should attempt it. Alternatively, we can follow the pavement downhill and around the hairpin bend at the gates to Kincragie, the ruined residence of the Earls of Shannon. A huge rhododendron dwarfs the gate lodge, and is resplendent in March.

Back at Courtmacsherry, we will find three welcoming pubs where in winter a warm fire and après-walk coffee, or Irish coffee, may be enjoyed. In summer, one may sit outside, or in the gardens of the hotel, and enjoy the evening peace over the bay.

***Note:** Re. Option C, more ambitious walkers, emerging onto the road above the southern end of Broad Strand may turn left, down the hill, where they will come to Coolbawn (also called Blind Strand). Here, the aforementioned 'Sprat Shoals Spectacular' is even more dramatic than at Broad Strand because the bay is very much narrower. The diversion adds no more than a mile.

Seven Heads Walk

An opportunity to enjoy the unspoiled beauty of the Seven Heads without arduous walking. Shanagh deserted village - Travarra Cove - cliffs and wild coastal scenery.

Locality: OS Sheet 87 Square 5137, the southern seaboard from Butlerstown, Co. Cork, to the sea. Courtmacsherry 3 miles, Timoleague 5, Clonakilty 8, Bandon 10.

Description and distance: A loop walk, 4.5 miles

Walking Time: 2 - 3 hrs

Walking conditions: Quiet back roads with hardly a car. A few medium-steep inclines. One stretch of rough field track - may be muddy.

Features: An exhilarating outing for walkers of all ages. Panoramic views over rolling, treeless country with Courtmacsherry Bay and Old Head of Kinsale to the east, Clonakilty Bay and Galley Head to the west. The open Atlantic. An abandoned village and a 'famine road'. Ring forts. Heather and gorse. Small, rocky coves, with pebble beaches. Wind-sculpted trees.

Flora and fauna: The coastal margin of the Seven Heads is depopulated and wild. Heather, ferns and gorse abound, rocks are splashed with brightly coloured lichens, walls are host to feather moss, wall rue, maidenhair spleenwort, hard ferns and hart's tongue ferns. Foxes, Irish hares, seals, peregrine falcons, merlins, choughs, ravens, cormorants, shags, gannets, guillemots, nesting fulmar, etc., any or all may be encountered. The rocks of the seashore are rich in shellfish, algae and sea anemones. From May to October, the rock pools teem with small fish and crustaceans.

Equipment: Any sensible shoes will do, but walkers should be warned that, after wet weather, the half mile long section of old roadway between fields can be churned by cattle and very muddy.

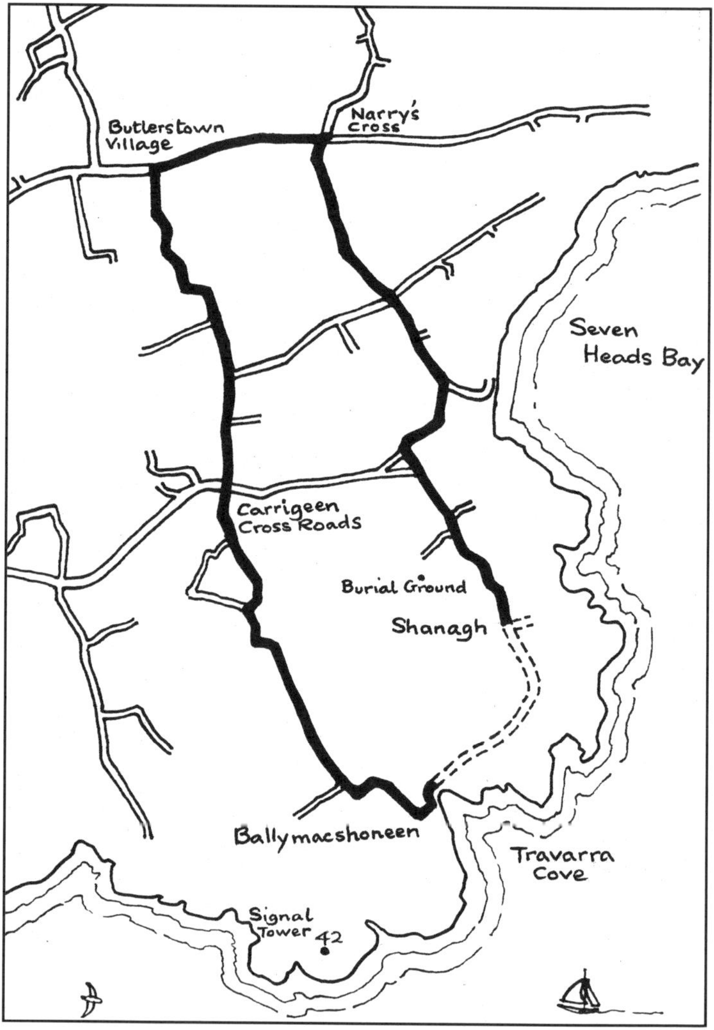

Walk No.5: Seven Heads. 2 to 3 hours. 4.5 miles

Itinerary

(1) Park the car at Narry's Cross (Grid Ref. 504389). To simplest way to find Narry's Cross is to drive through Butlerstown from the west (houses and shops on the left), pass the Community Hall (on the left) and continue for a half mile to the brown signpost saying "Timoleague. Coast Road. 10km". This is Narry's Cross. There is a triangle of grass between the roads where one may park.

From Narry's Cross one can see the route, straight ahead, downhill towards the open Atlantic, which is roughly 2 miles distant. Pause to enjoy the180° view of the broad, green landscape dotted with scattered farms and a few trees. To the right (the west) lies the Galley Head, with its lighthouse, the westerly arm of Dunworley Bay. Set off down the road towards the sea.

A lone cottage on the right, with a few wind-torn trees for shelter. Continue straight across the four-cross-roads. To the left may be seen a modern slate-faced, pink confectioned house, unusual in this countryside for its large size, design and affluence, symbol of the new Ireland and the success that may be achieved by the enterprising local man, even in remote areas such as this.

This was once Poor Law land, and the simple, bare farmhouses, the ruins and stone-walled fields attest the bitter struggle for mere subsistence. Times have changed. Where there are ruins, there is a stranger to buy and renovate them. The wild coast that reminds the native of famine and emigration seems to the misanthropic city dweller a haven from stress, traffic, people, a landscape where spirit-nurturing Nature still rules supreme.

Continue downhill. An old farmhouse across fields to the left, with a wind-torn macracapra pine in front. This is windy country, with "sceac" bushes (blackthorns) like bonsai growing out of the low stone walls, sculpted into tortured shapes by the south westerlies sweeping in from the coast in winter storms. Hart's tongue ferns on the stone walls along the lane are salt burnt, although still nearly half a mile from the sea.

(2) A "Y" in the road, where a stream passes under via a culvert. The left leg of the Y plunges down to a cove, while the right leg continues our route and climbs steeply towards the sky. Divert to the cove for a few minutes; it is worthwhile. The lane follows the stream, gushing down a deep, ferny ravine, and descends steeply to a small, pebble beach, with a short slipway and a concrete path leading across sea-rock outcrops to a platform, suitable for docking boats or for swimmers to dive off in summer.

It is a lonely place, rarely visited. Acorn barnacles, seed mussels , limpets, periwinkles, whelks and sea anemones are everywhere on the rocks. From March to October, the rock pools are full of life, miniature, perfect aquariums, resplendent with red coralline, green sea lettuce, yellow carragheen moss. Small, highly specialised fish like shannies, blennies and rockling hide in the clear depths, along with many species of prawns, crabs, starfish and brittle stars.

Old Head Of Kinsale seen from Coolim Cliffs

The lone house above the cove must enjoy one of the finest views in Ireland, looking out across Courtmacsherry Bay to the distant beaches of Garretstown and the cliffs of the Old Head of Kinsale. From the laneway approaching it, one may share this view.

Returning to the main route, one now climbs a few hundred yards of steep road, passing a neat, well kept farmhouse. Far behind us, Courtmacsherry Bay; ahead Clonakilty Bay, and the Galley Head. At the top of the hill, we follow the track that follows the wall around to the left, past a field gate. This high point commands 360° views. Two miles to the north, across wide, rich fields, is the village of Butlerstown, its single street of multicoloured houses facing us. To the south, is the wide Atlantic, reflecting a blue sky or lit by magic, silvery light diffusing through the clouds. To the east, Courtmacsherry Bay, bounded by the distant cliffs of the Old Head. To the west, in the middle distance, the coves of Dunworley, white surf breaking on dark rocks, with small sandy beaches in between.

We continue, following the wall on the left side of the track, and join the paved road again after thirty yards. Our route now leads straight for the sea.

Ignore the road on the right, going west to Carigeen Cross Roads. On each side, Connemara-style stone walls, patterned with white lichen, divide sizeable, rolling fields. The stones, cleared from the land long ago, had to be put somewhere, and served a useful purpose for building walls. To the right is a track marked on the OS map, leading to old Burial Grounds. It passes through a farmyard and is much used by cattle. It is a quagmire in wet weather and cannot be negotiated with less that rubber boots.

At the end of the paved road, we reach the ruins of Shanagh, a grey village of eleven or so stone houses that never knew plaster or paint. Some are large; all but one were abandoned until recently. It is an ancient settlement, its name deriving from seantoir, the Irish for sanctuarium, referring to a church or burial ground the memory of which has been preserved in the name for some thirteen hundred years. The burial ground is close by.

During the Great Famine of 1845-48 , one third of the population of Shanagh died. Many, abandoning their homes and disease-devastated potato crops, dragged their starved bodies ten miles to Clonakilty Workhouse where, if they were lucky, they were registered as paupers and taken into care. More often, there was no room or food and they joined the many like them who came from all over West Cork and died in the streets of Clonakilty. "Where are the owners of this cabin gone?", a stranger might ask a neighbour during those desperate years. "To Clonakilty, God help us!" was too often the reply. Clonakilty, a prosperous town, became synonymous with a pauper's death. The population of Shanagh in 1841 was 91; by 1851, it was 61. Until thirty years ago, eleven houses were still occupied and there was a shop. Its population is just one family, today.

A band of choughs in flight

(3) Find the track leaving the village between the ruins to the right. There is a track to the left but it is a quagmire, and comes to a dead end in a field. The track we follow is a surviving section of a "famine road", leading from the nearby hamlet of Ballinluig to Coostravarra (Travarra Cove), a "public works" project set up in 1847 to provide famine relief in return for work, thus to obviate outright charity and the perceived ills that would attend. Men on the verge of starvation, barely able to stand, queued for jobs. Fr. James Coombes, local historian and the present parish priest of Timoleague, records the case of one Patrick Murray, sole supporter of a wife and six children who, having subsisted on nothing but a few turnips for several days, died after one day's labour. This old road may be extremely muddy in winter; it is much used by cattle, and is poorly drained.

This famine road leads through stone-walled fields towards the sea. Off to the right, we see a Signal Tower erected in1804-06,.and two observation posts looking out to sea. This tower is within view of towers to the east, at the Old Head, and to the west, at Galley Head. The idea was to ring the south coast with a communications system for fear the French would again invade, as they had in 1796 and 1798.

History records that, in the 1840's, a pier was built at Travarra Cove, also as part of the Famine Relief Programme. Only a short boat slip is to be seen today. It is hard to believe that a pier would last long in the massive seas that wash into Travarra in winter.

On the 13th of January, 1925, a large vessel, The Cardiff Hall, on the last lap of its voyage from Argentina to Cork with a cargo of maize, ran aground on the vicious Shoonta Rock off Travarra Cove, with the loss of all 27 souls aboard. Only two bodies were recovered, that of the Welsh captain and an Arab seaman. The lifeboat, now stationed at Courtmacsherry but then at Barry's Point, was launched; however, the fierceness of the gale made it impossible to row around the point to bring assistance. So wild was the sea that a piece of wreckage weighing two tons was thrown forty feet above the tide. A vast quantity of 'yellow meal' was washed ashore, bringing people from all over the hinterland to collect it. Temporary mills were set up at Butlerstown to grind and sell the grain, while trawlers worked for months recovering it from the sea bed. The anchor of the Cardiff Hall was brought ashore in 1987 and is exhibited on the grass verge at the western end of Courtmacsherry (see Courtmacsherry Walk).

(4) A small stream issues onto the pebble beach at Travarra, but the track (cleared marked on the OS map) that once followed its eastern bank and met the paved road east of Carrigeen Cross Roads in now impassable. Instead, we cross the stream and take the road that climbs from the boat slip. An old winch stands in the hedge on the right, rusted and decaying. On the other side of the stream, a few stones-upon-stones mark the ruins of an ancient cottage. The village of Butlerstown, two miles off, is framed in the 'vee' of the craggy, gorse-grown ravine down which the stream runs. At the top of the hill, an abandoned car rots in a field, not a pretty sight, with, beyond it, a farmhouse. The farmyard's contents - high-and-dry boats, lobster pots, and fishing gear - attest to the farmer's diverse trades. The farmyard opposite is full of old fridges and washing machines, an unedifying sight in this attractive landscape.

Travarra Cove, Seven Heads

We are now in the town land and hamlet of Ballymacshoneen. The name 'Shoneen' is derogatory in some parts of Ireland, meaning the person so called is a turncoat, a 'West Brit'. It may come from "Seánín" or "Seáneen", meaning "little Seán", perhaps implying a pandering Paddy, kept by the Big House as a cute, forelock-touching, domestic pet. However, the Ballymacshoneen people were far from pandering, and the very landscape they lived in demanded independence and fortitude to survive.

The old roadside pump delivers sweet water and tested nitrate-free in December 1997, although nitrate traces, from fertiliser run-off, showed in most local ground water at that time. However, drink it at your own risk! It is faintly flavoured with iron oxide, a not unpleasant tang.

The road now leads straight for pretty Butlerstown, a line of colourful houses facing us about two miles away. The roadside walls are fecund with lichens, hard fern, hart's tongue, navelworth and small, flowering succulents.

This is a land of ancient ring forts, with seven identified between Shanagh and Dunworley alone. In a field to the left of the road is a well preserved

Great black slug, common on the coastal margin

example, about 100 feet in diameter, with encircling ramparts rising four or five feet above the sward. These forts proliferated on the landscape in the early Christian period, the fifth to the tenth century. The perimeter banks marked farmyards, not fortresses, the wooden structures inside having long since decayed. The earth works are brown with dead ferns and gorse in winter, bright green and orange in summer, with the whiff of coconut rising from the gorse. It is well that so many of these early settlements are still preserved. We owe it to the 'fairies'. The country belief that these were fairy forts or 'pookeen raths' protected them from the plough.

(5) Approaching Carrigeen Cross Roads, views to the left reveal Dunworley coves and bay, and are especially lovely in the evening when the sun sets beyond them, to the west. We cross Carrigeen Cross Roads diametrically; the route is now quite clear, the road visible ahead. "Carrigeen" means Little Rock, nothing to do with the Arkansas town or with Carragheen Moss, the sea weed harvested from time immemorial by the Irish, one of the few sea vegetables exploited by our conservative race. It is health-giving and, when we had tummy bugs as children, my mother made it into a greyish-white blancmange, easy on the stomach but hardly attractive to the eye. We ate it under protest. I'm sure there must be better recipes; I shall consult the Japanese

(6) At the village 'street', we turn immediately right, and pass the Community Hall before walking the last half mile on the high road back to Narry's Cross and the car. This is a fine road for views, with a rich, green sward of grasslands stretching to the broad Atlantic and solid farmhouses dotting the land.

Should we be in no hurry home, Butlerstown village affords a fine welcome for the thirsty walker. Its two pubs, O'Regan's and O'Neill's, each equally welcoming, are family concerns, the cosy interiors of which have changed little in half a century. In the afternoons and early evenings, they are quiet places. In summer, one can almost hear the motes of dust falling in the sunlight. Or the coal stir in the winter fire.

Notes